FREEHAND

SKETCHBOOK SERIES 1
ADULT COLORING BOOK

Printed in the United States of America

First Printing, 2016

Illustrated by: Savana Ellison

first of many.

thank you.

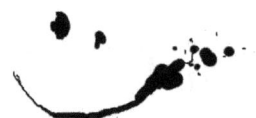

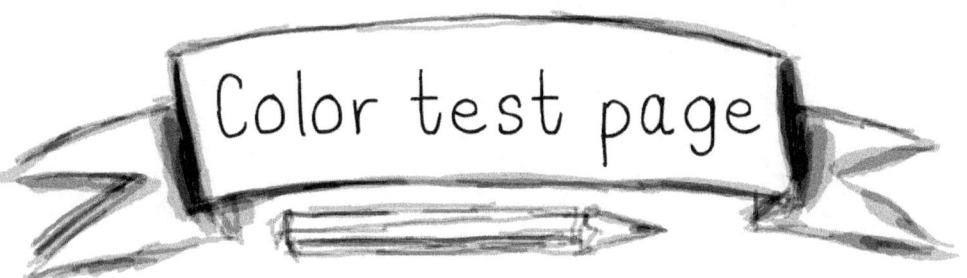

Color test page

Believe

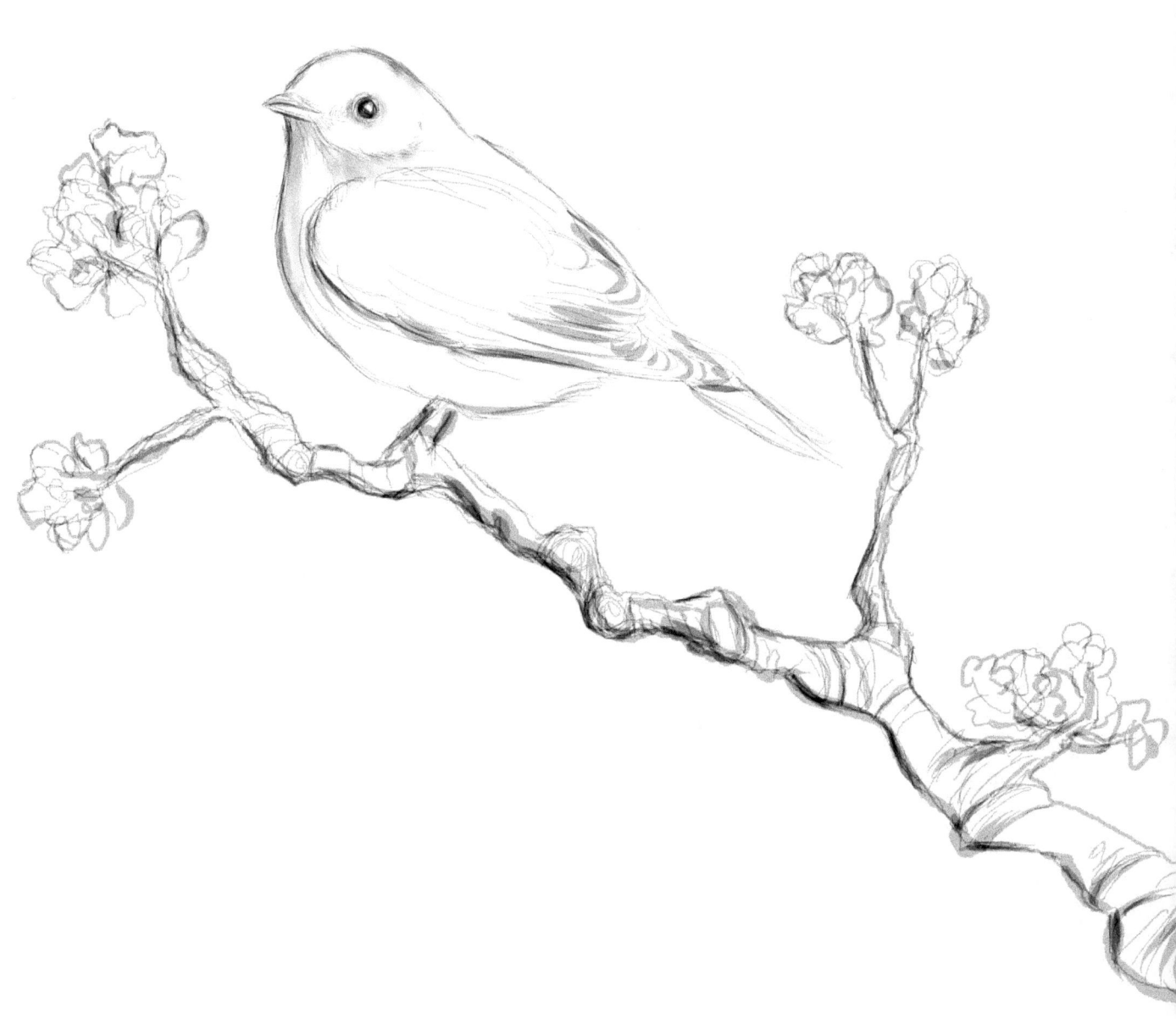

Believe

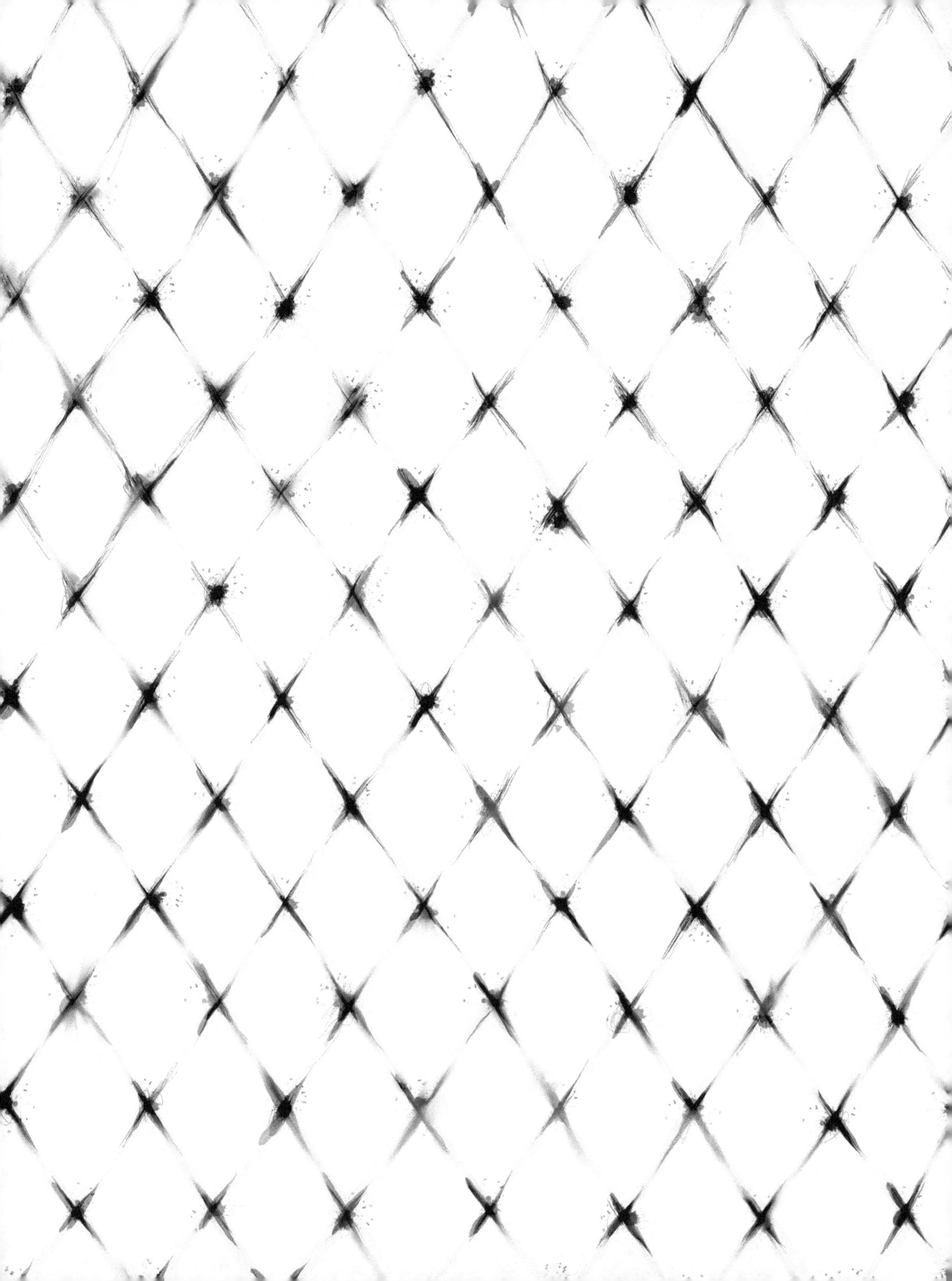

Believe

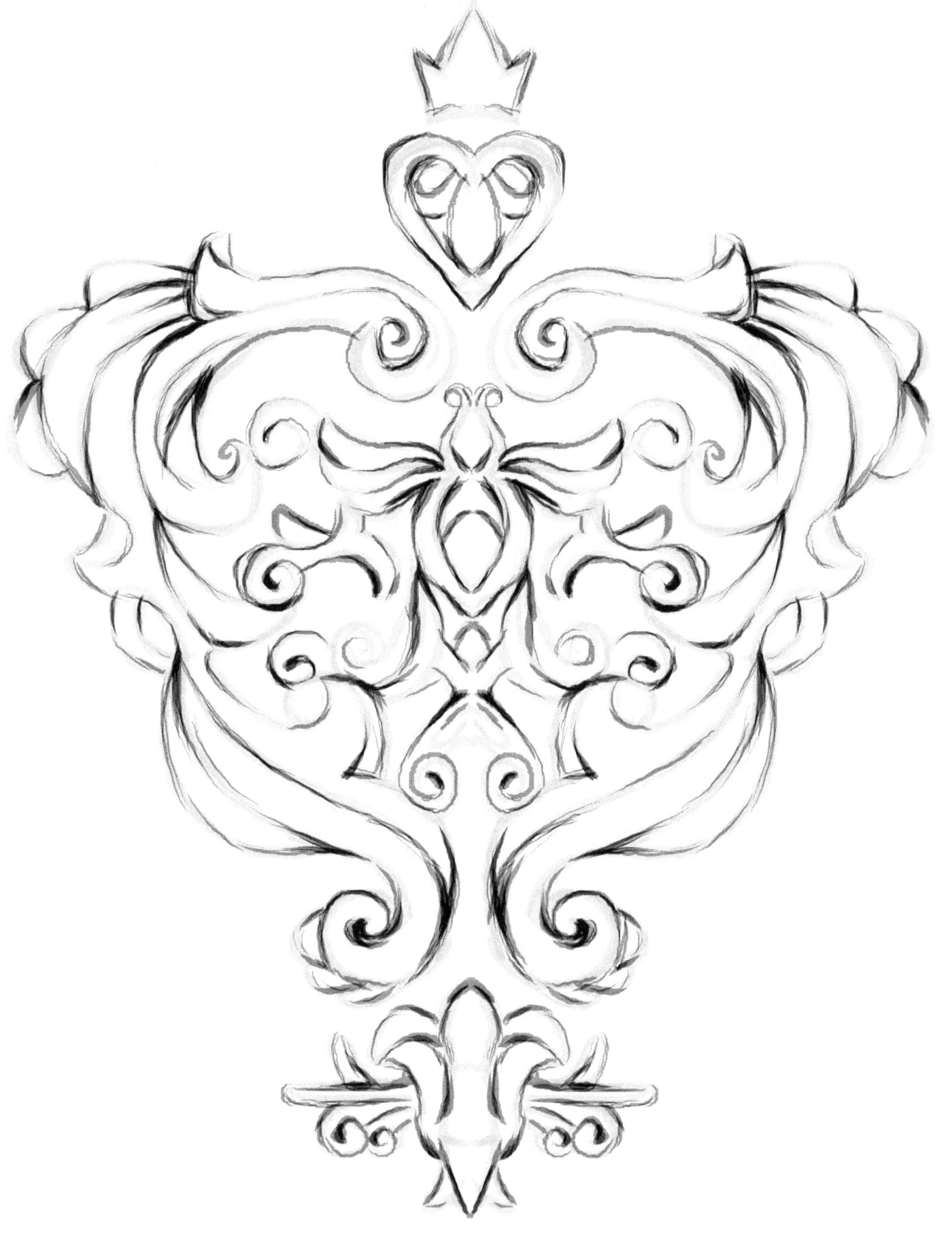

Believe

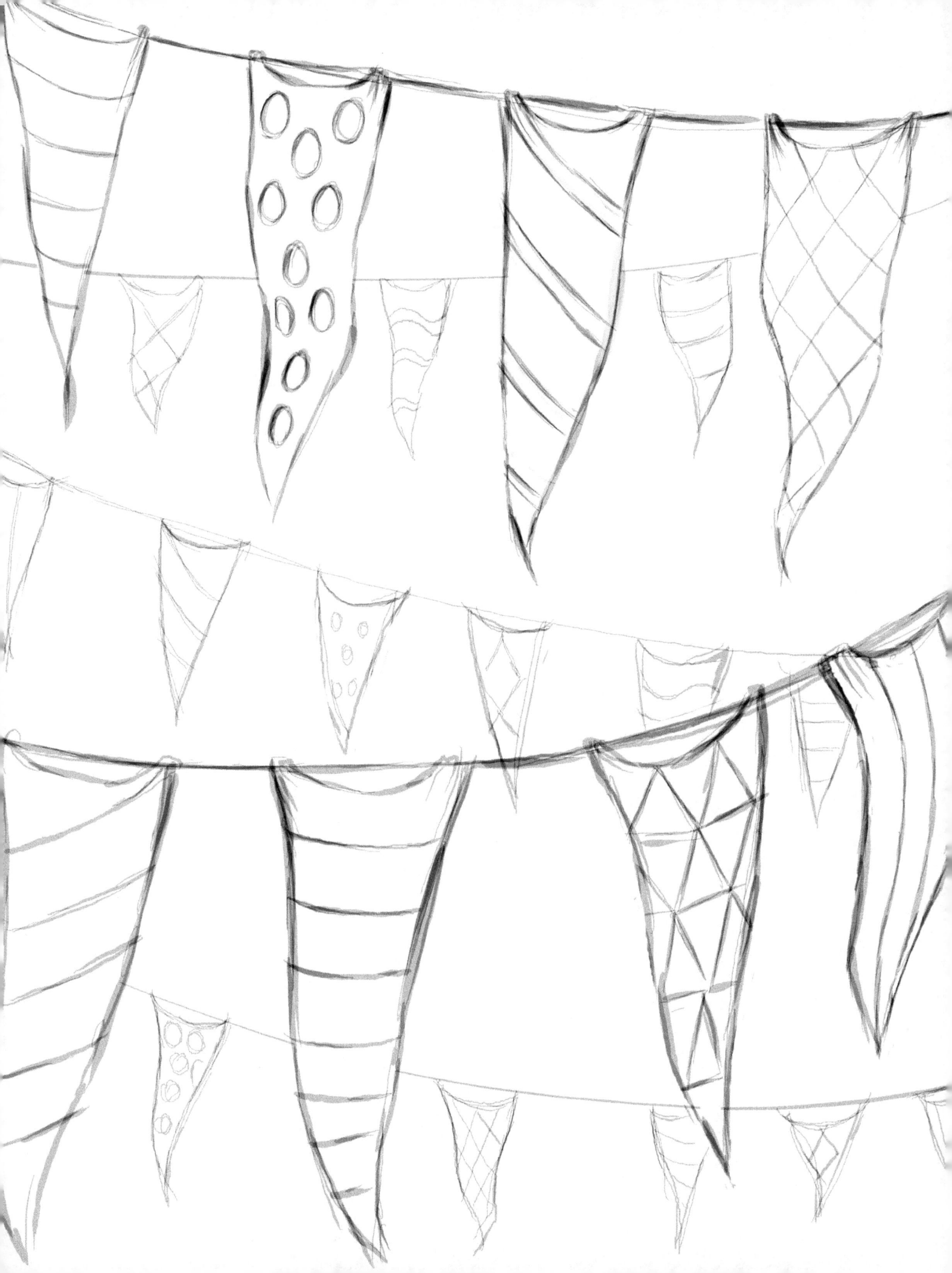

Believe

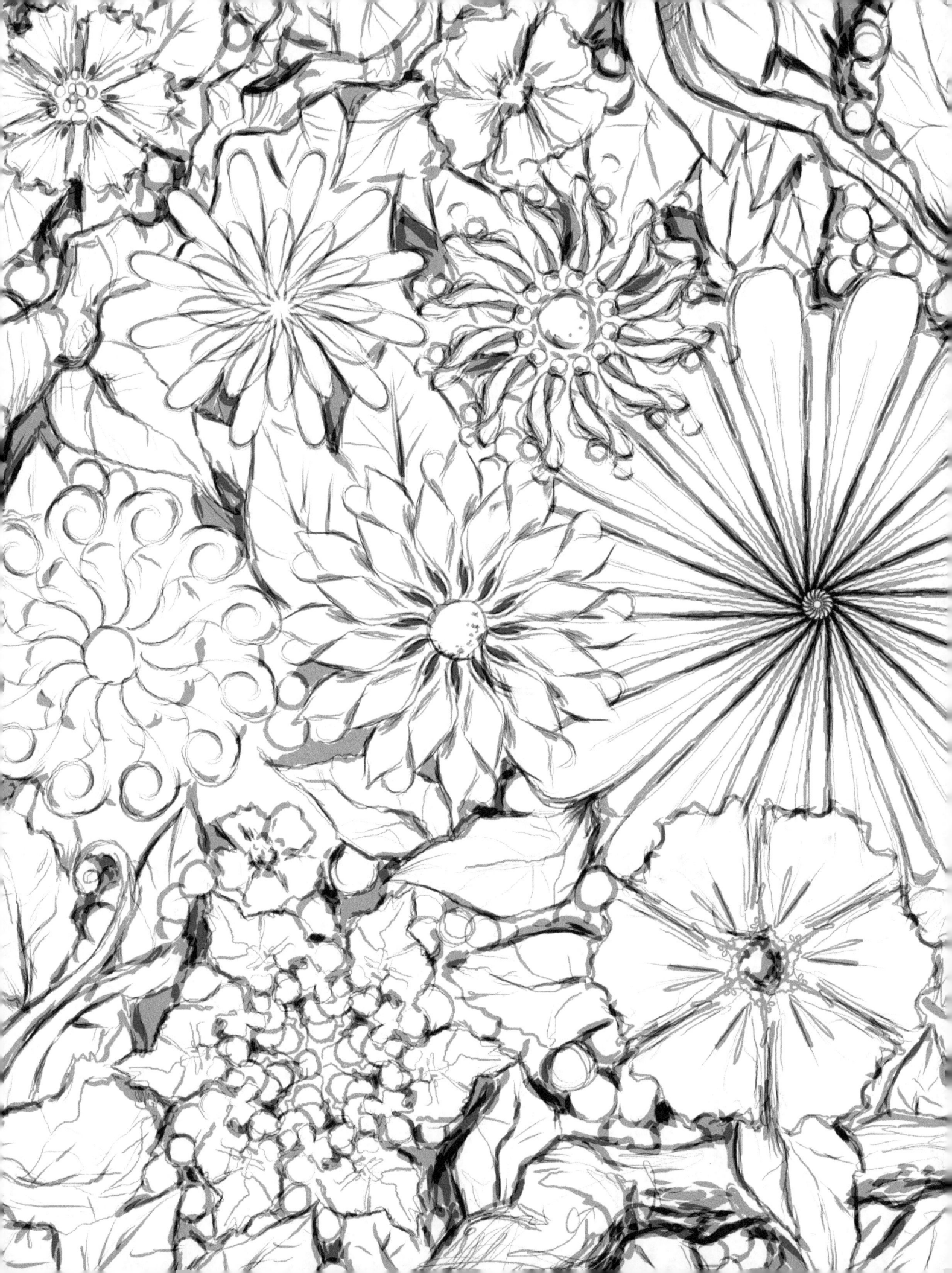

Believe

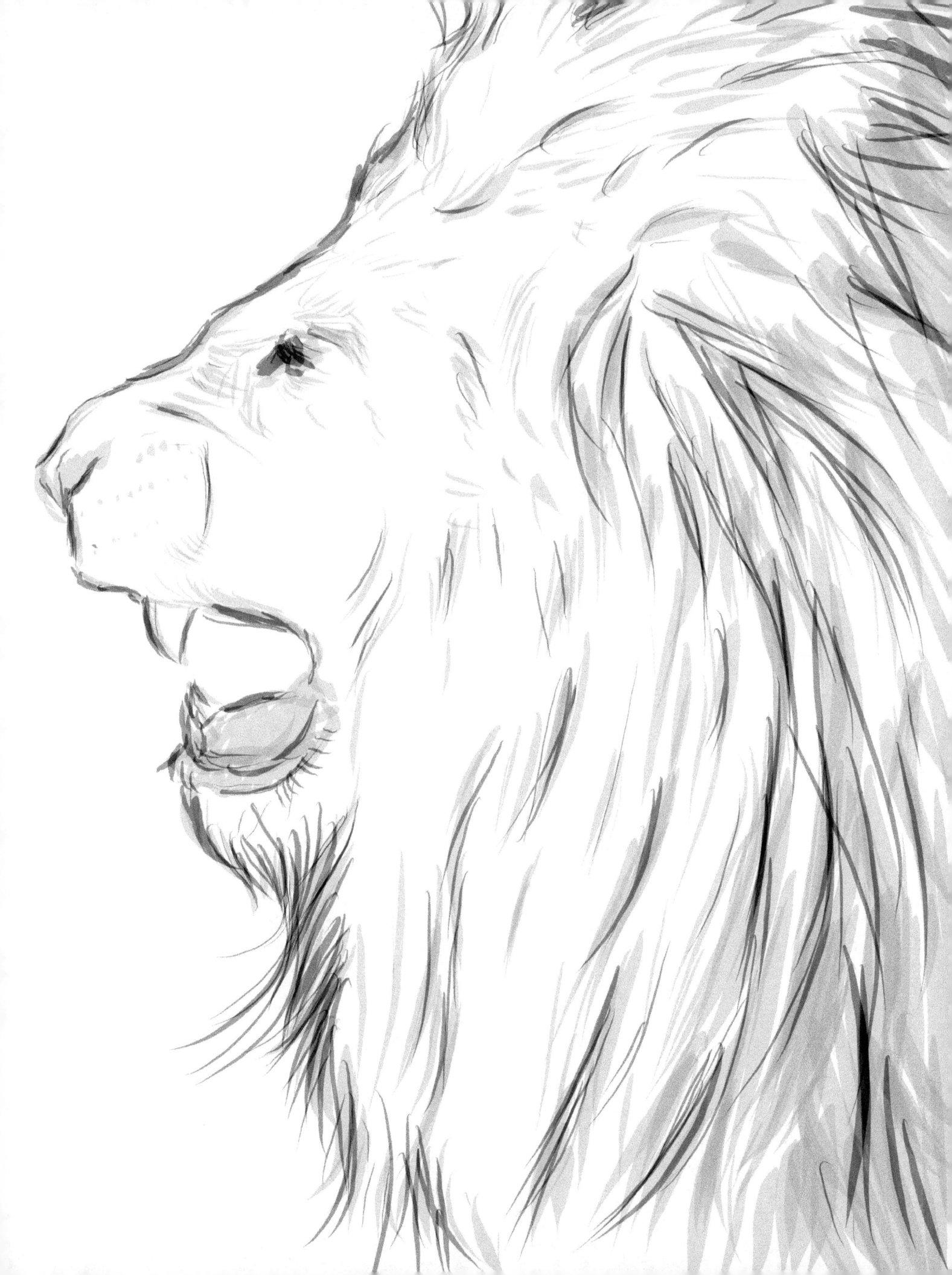

Believe

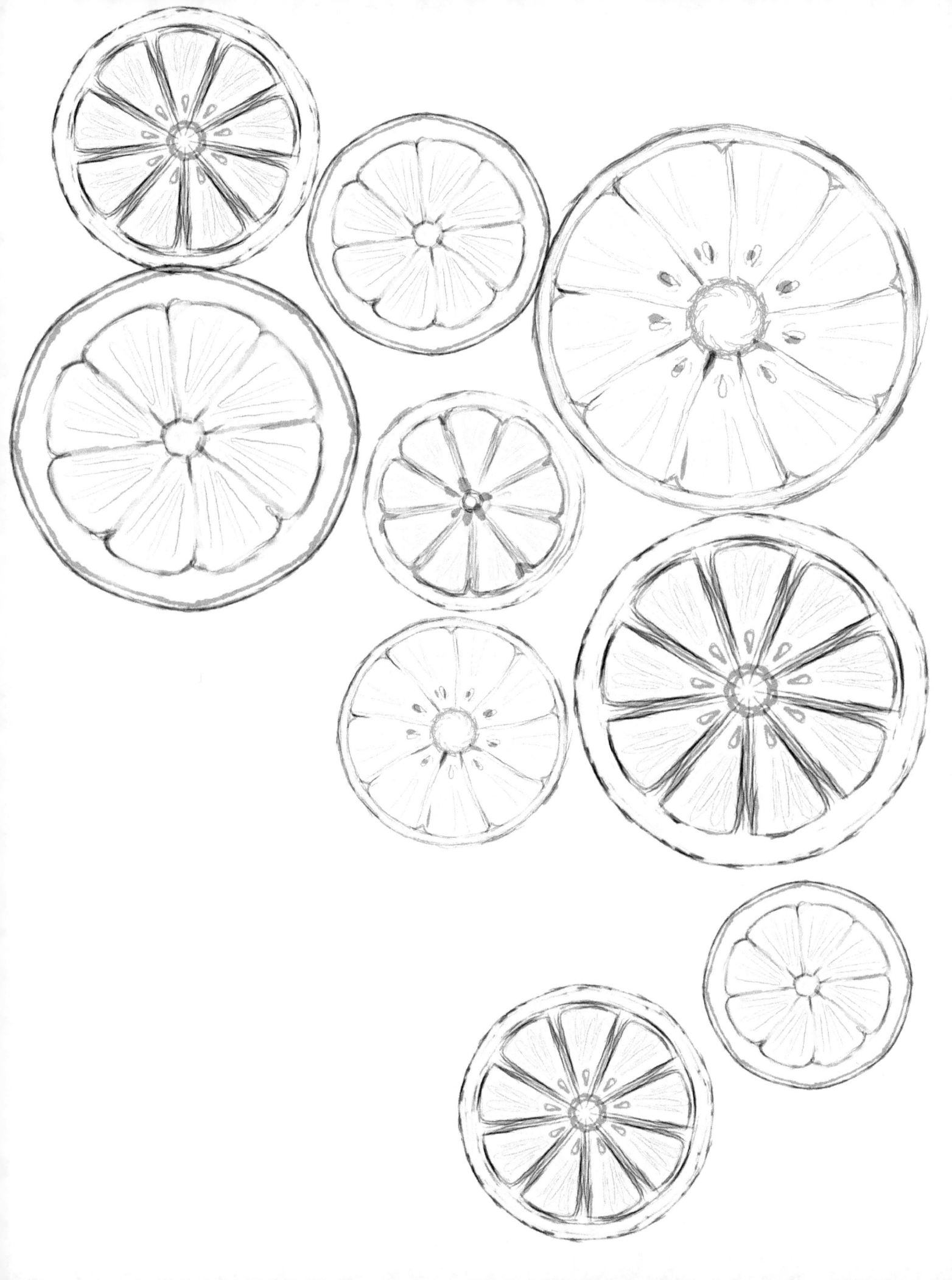

Believe

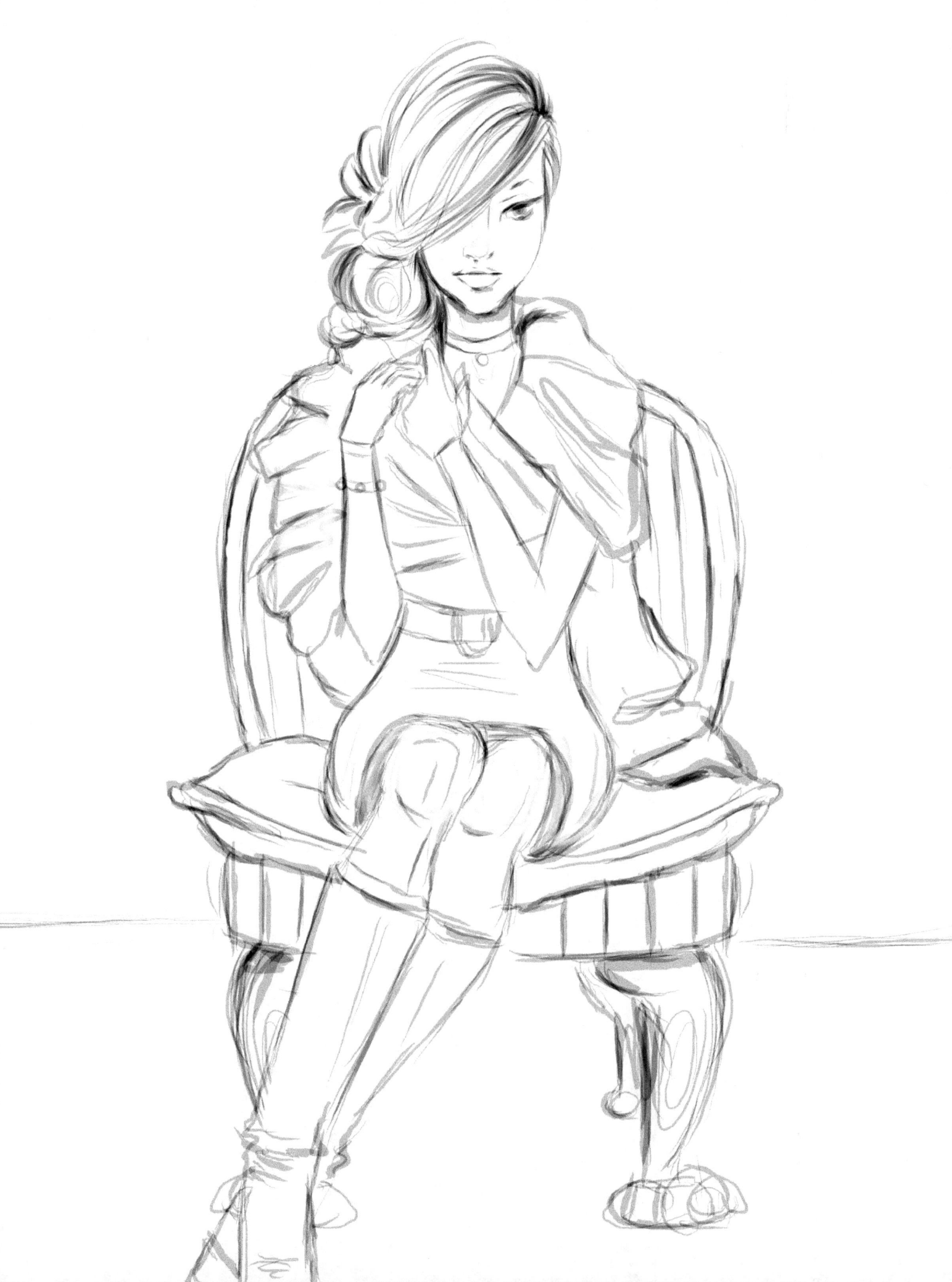

Believe

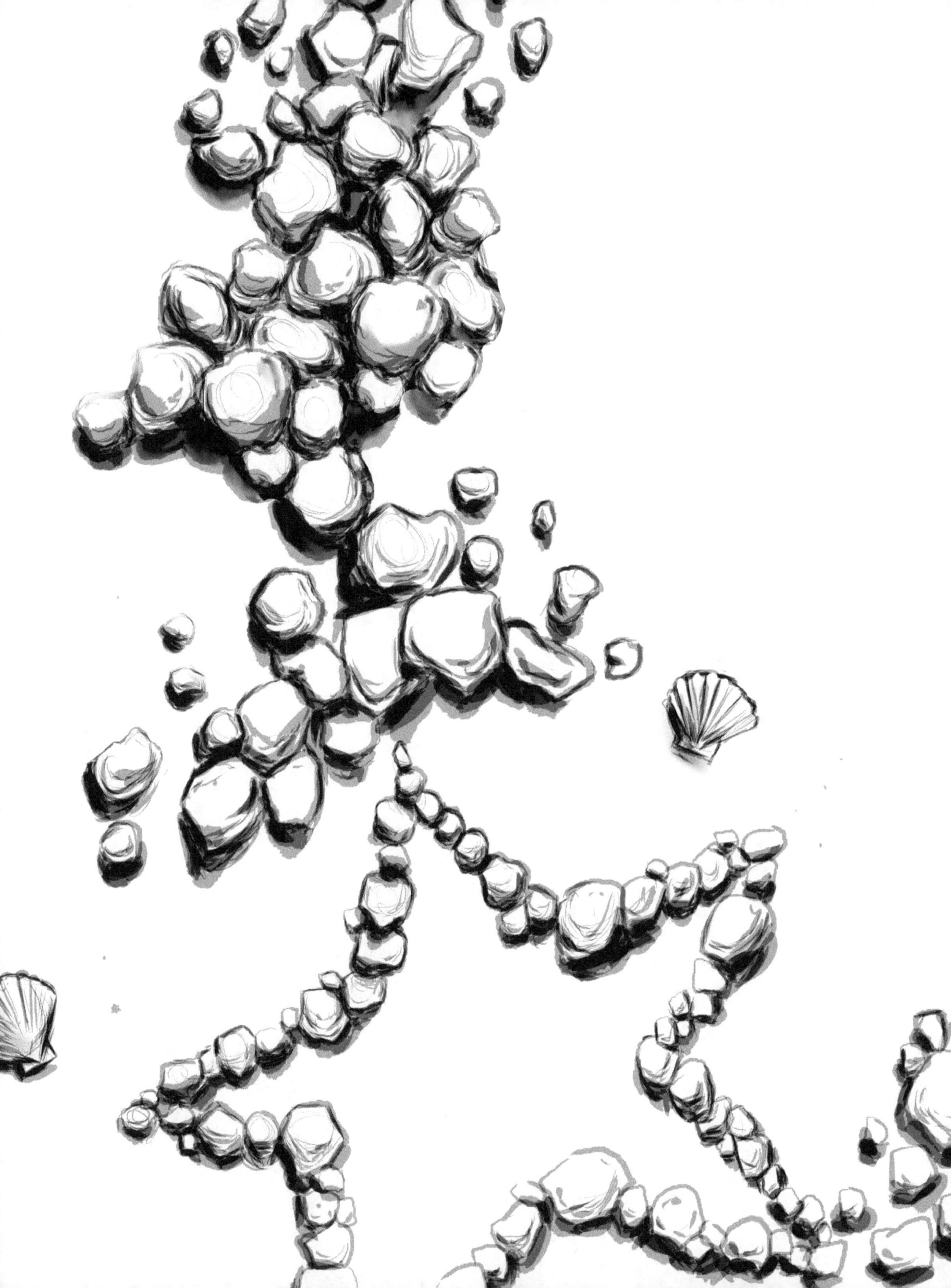

Believe

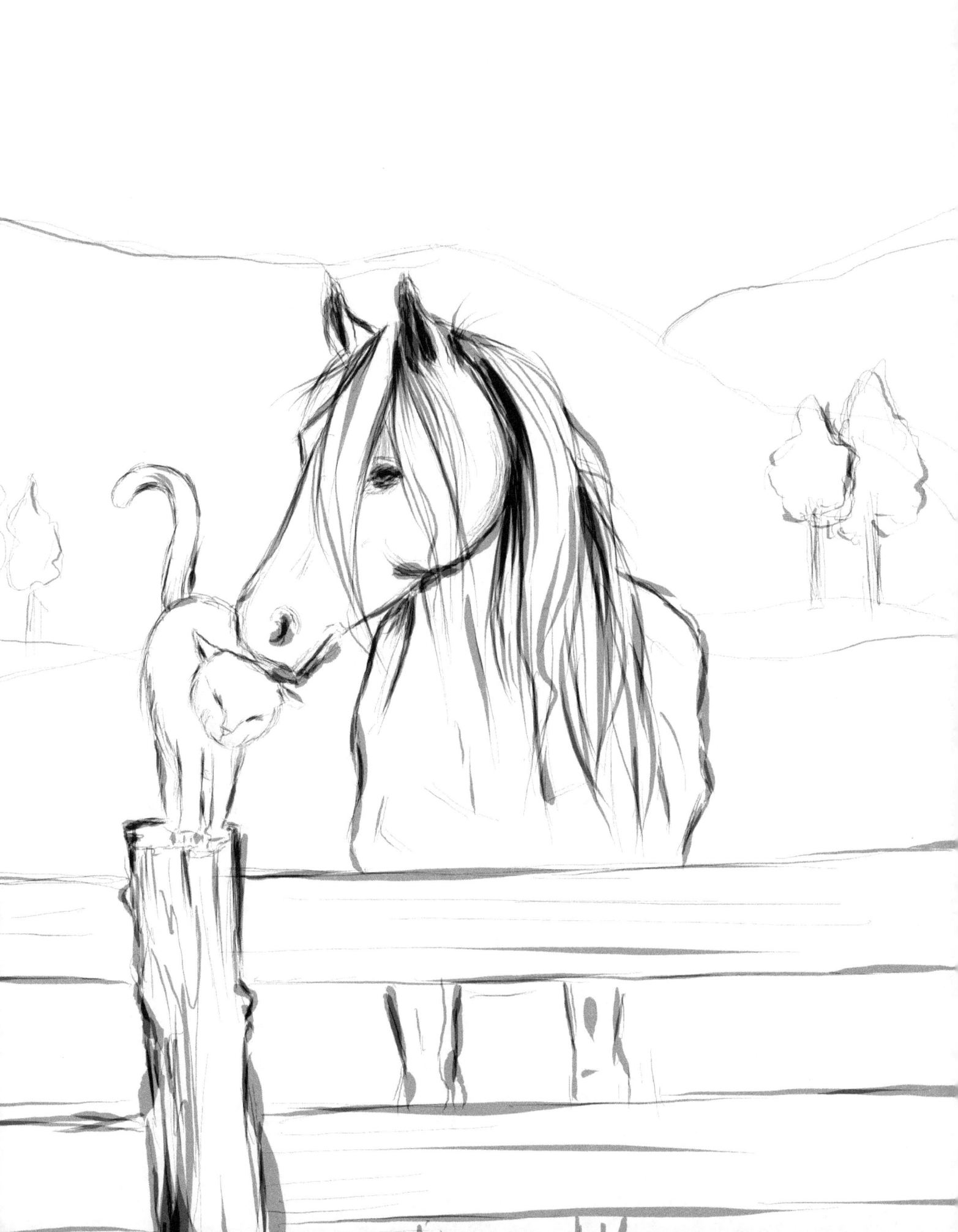

Believe

abcdfe

hiklm

norstu

jgpqy

vwxz

Believe

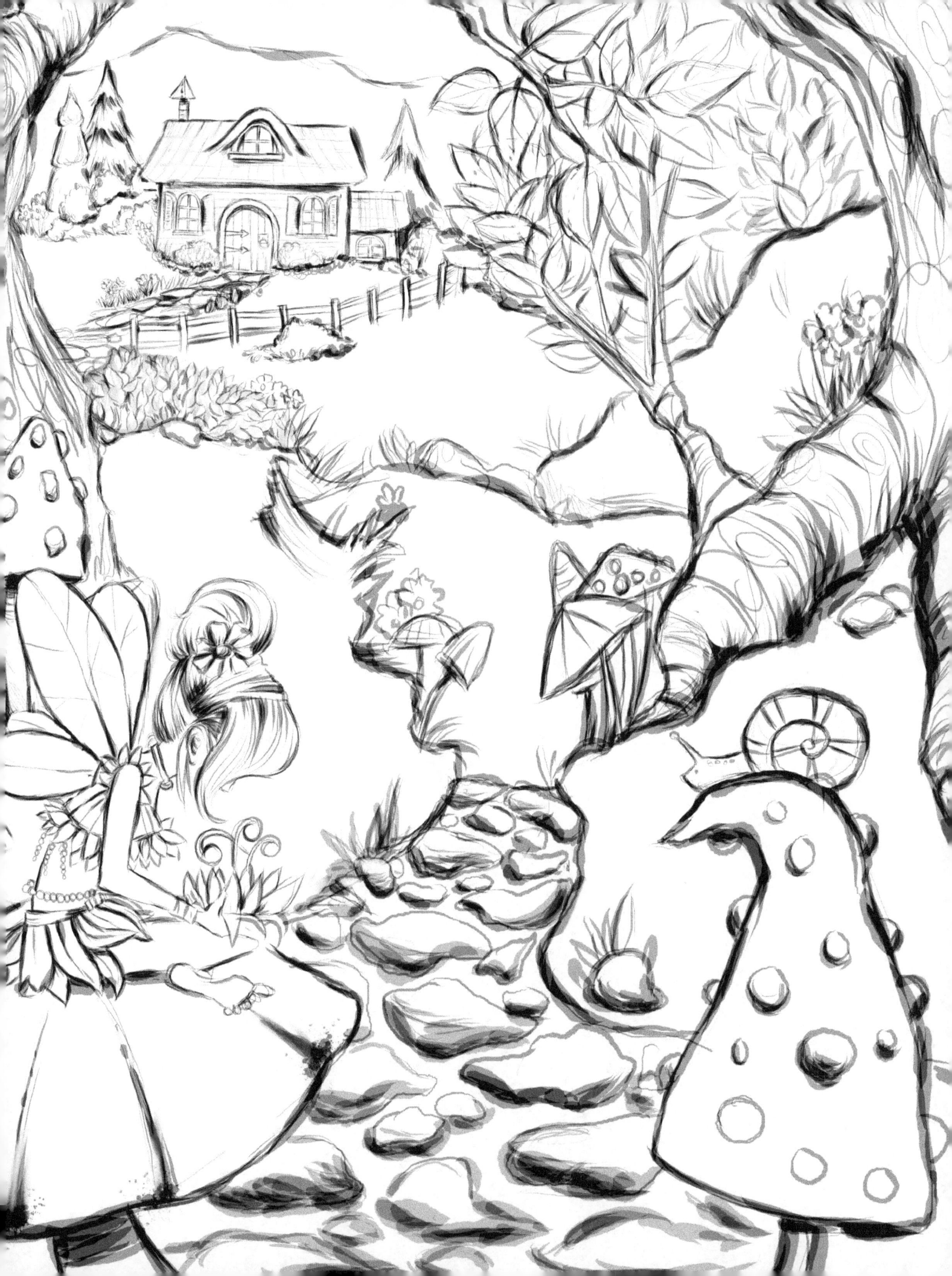

Believe

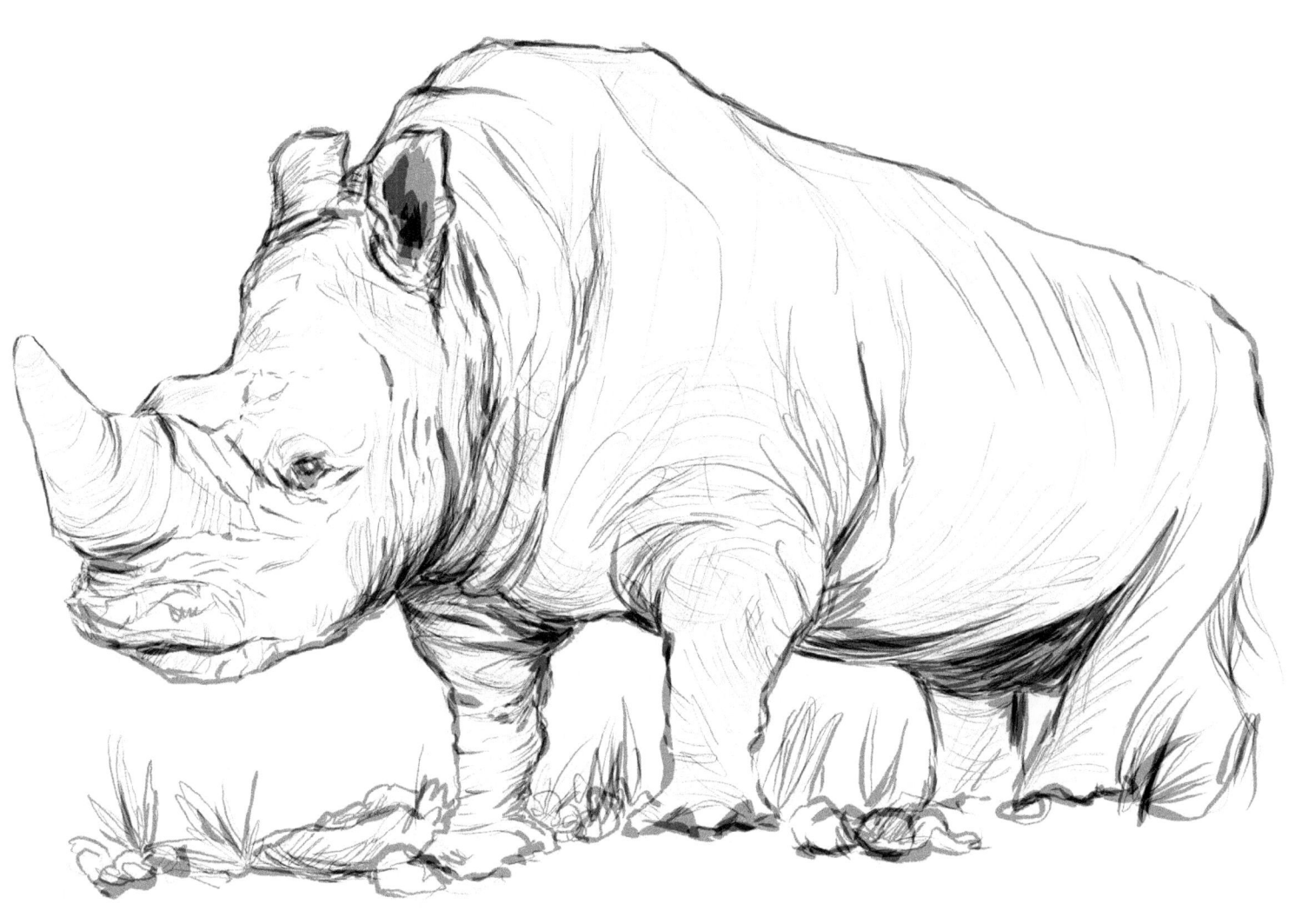

Believe

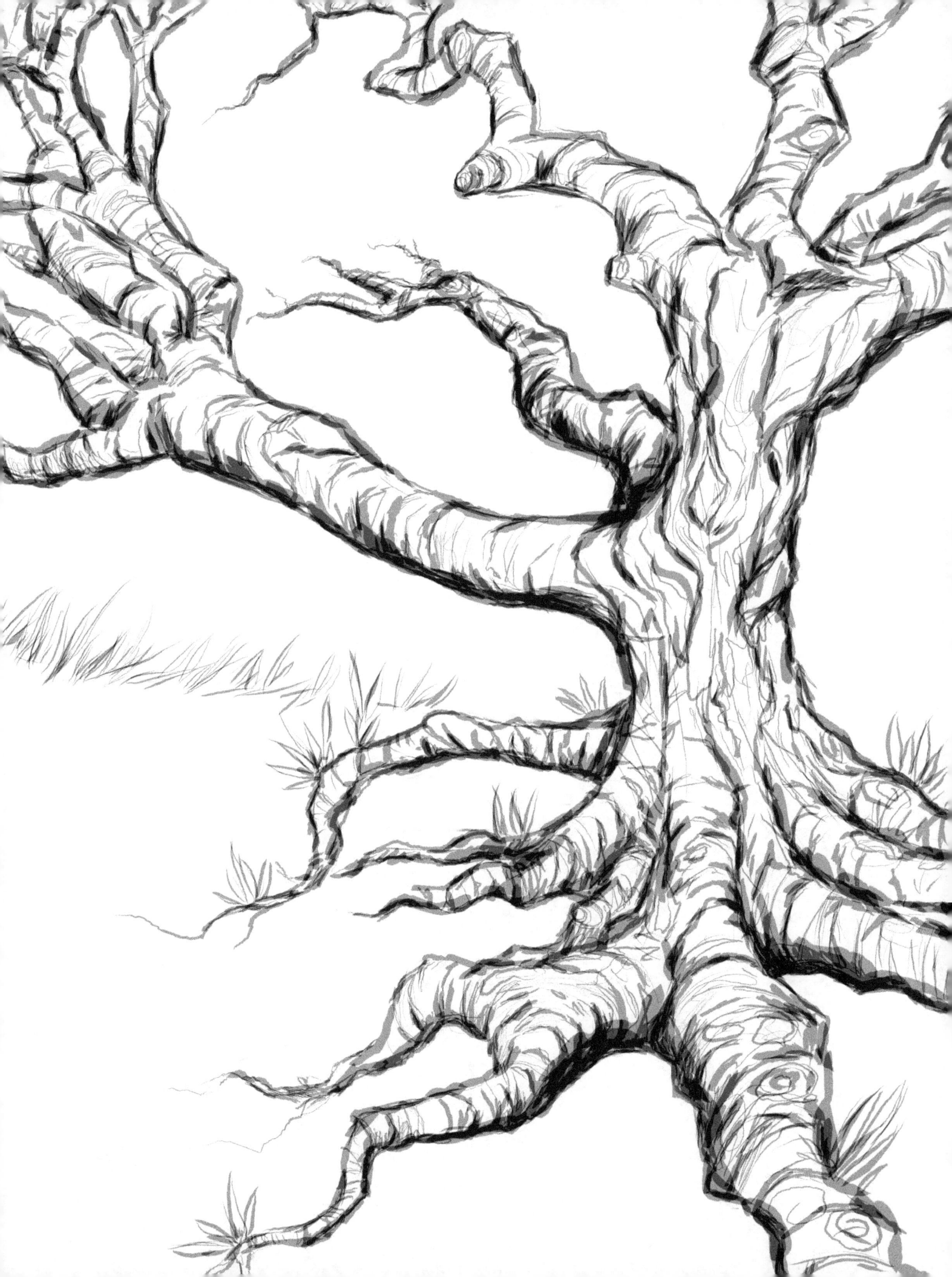

Believe

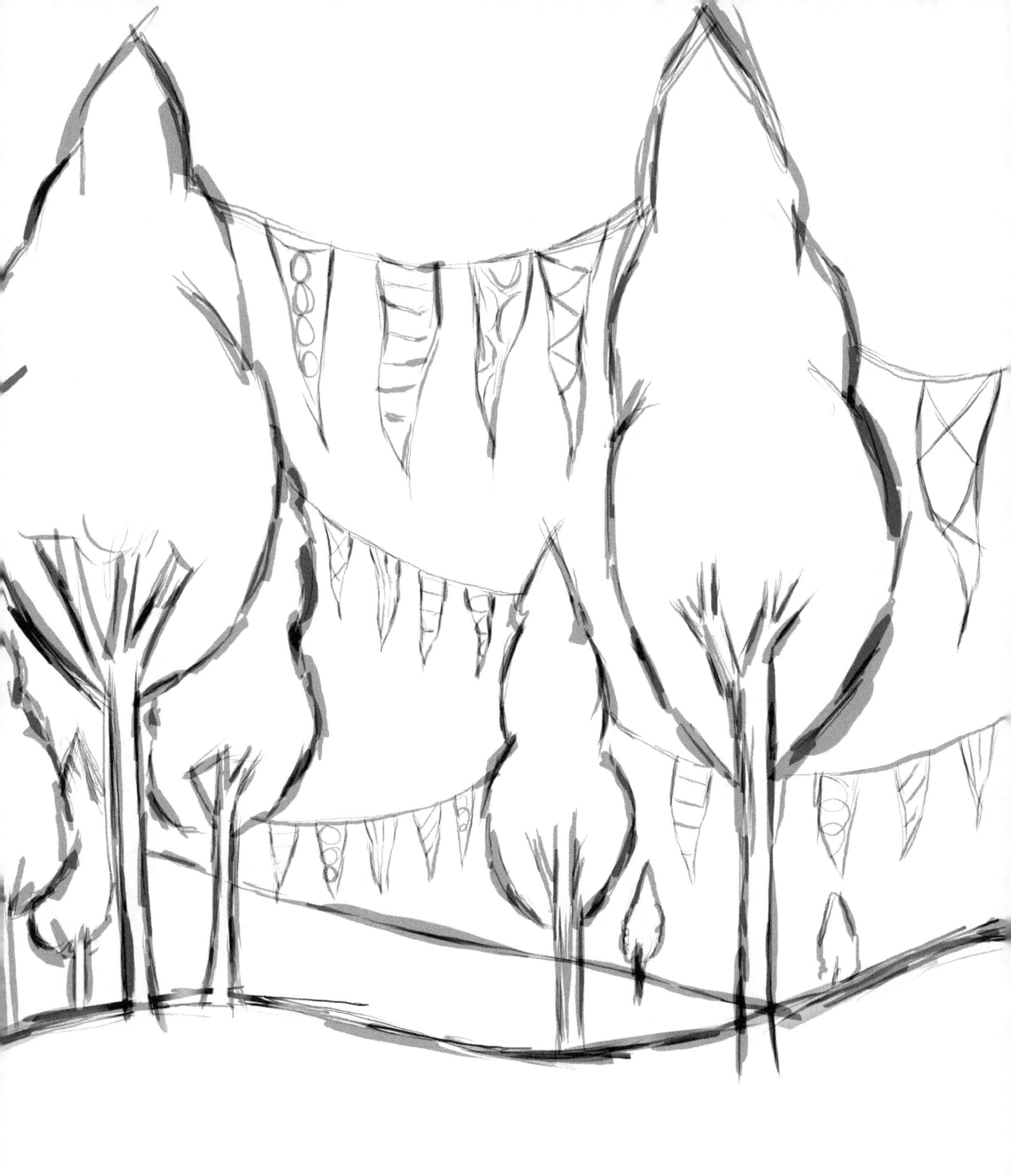

Believe

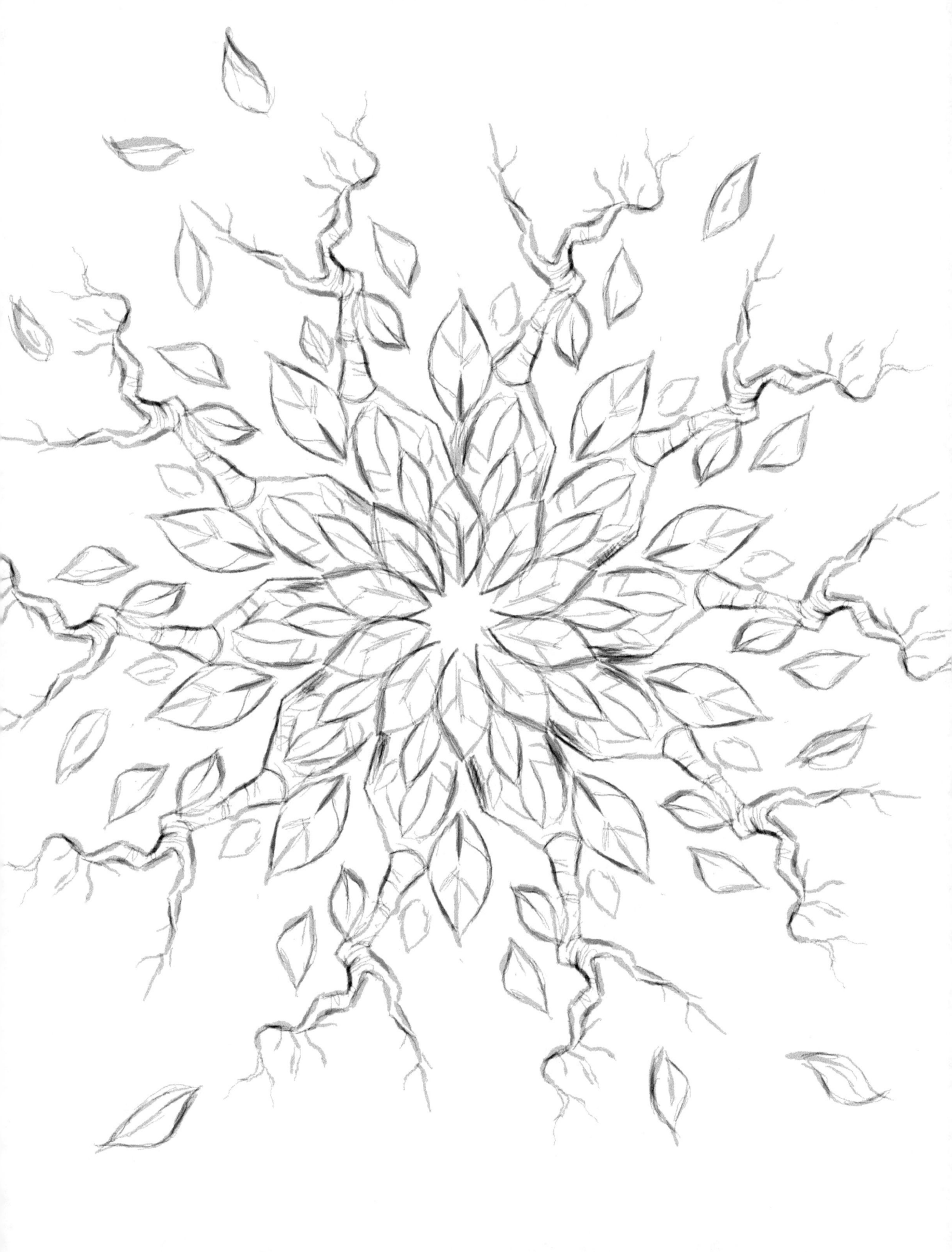

Believe

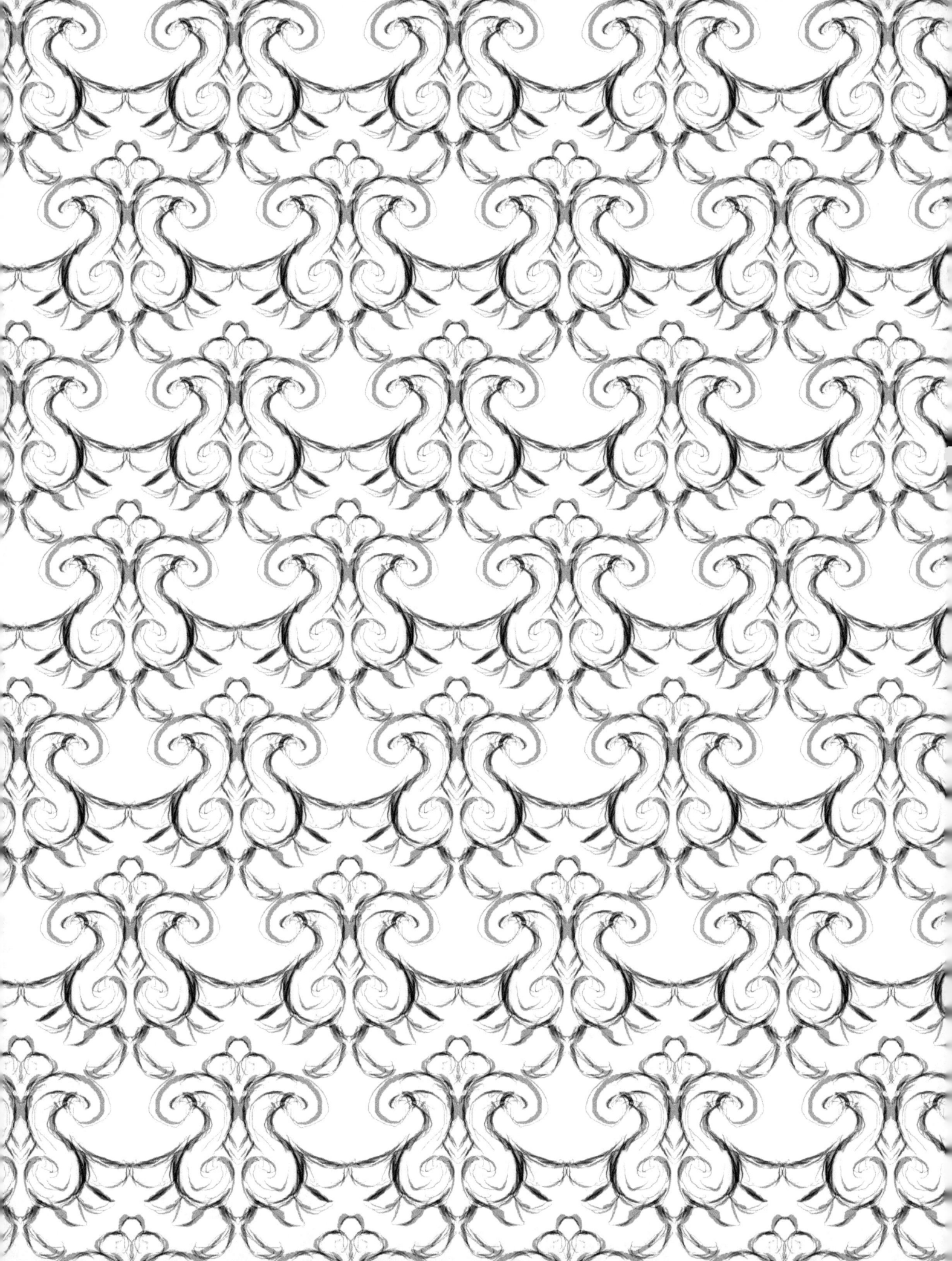

Believe

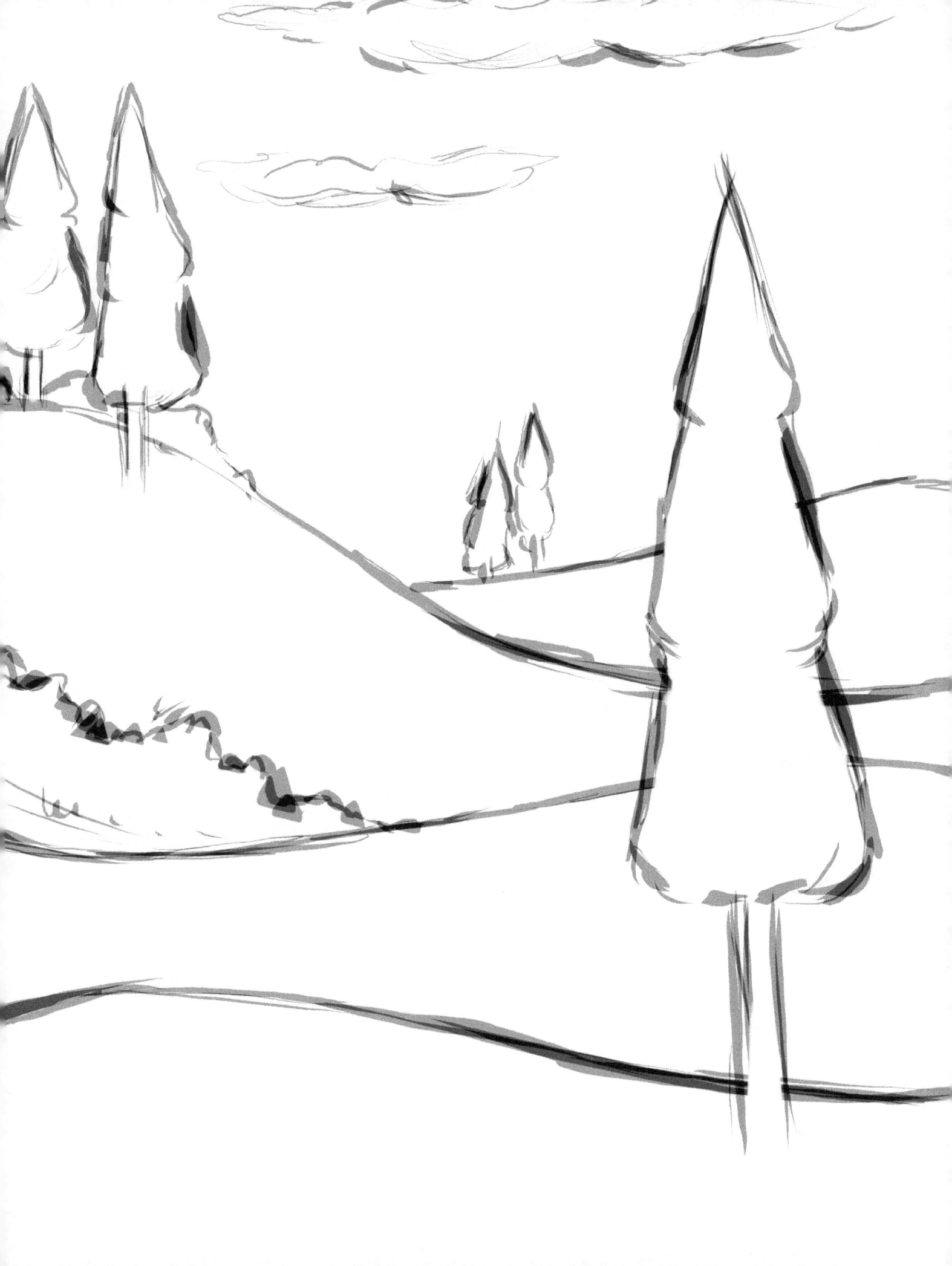

Believe

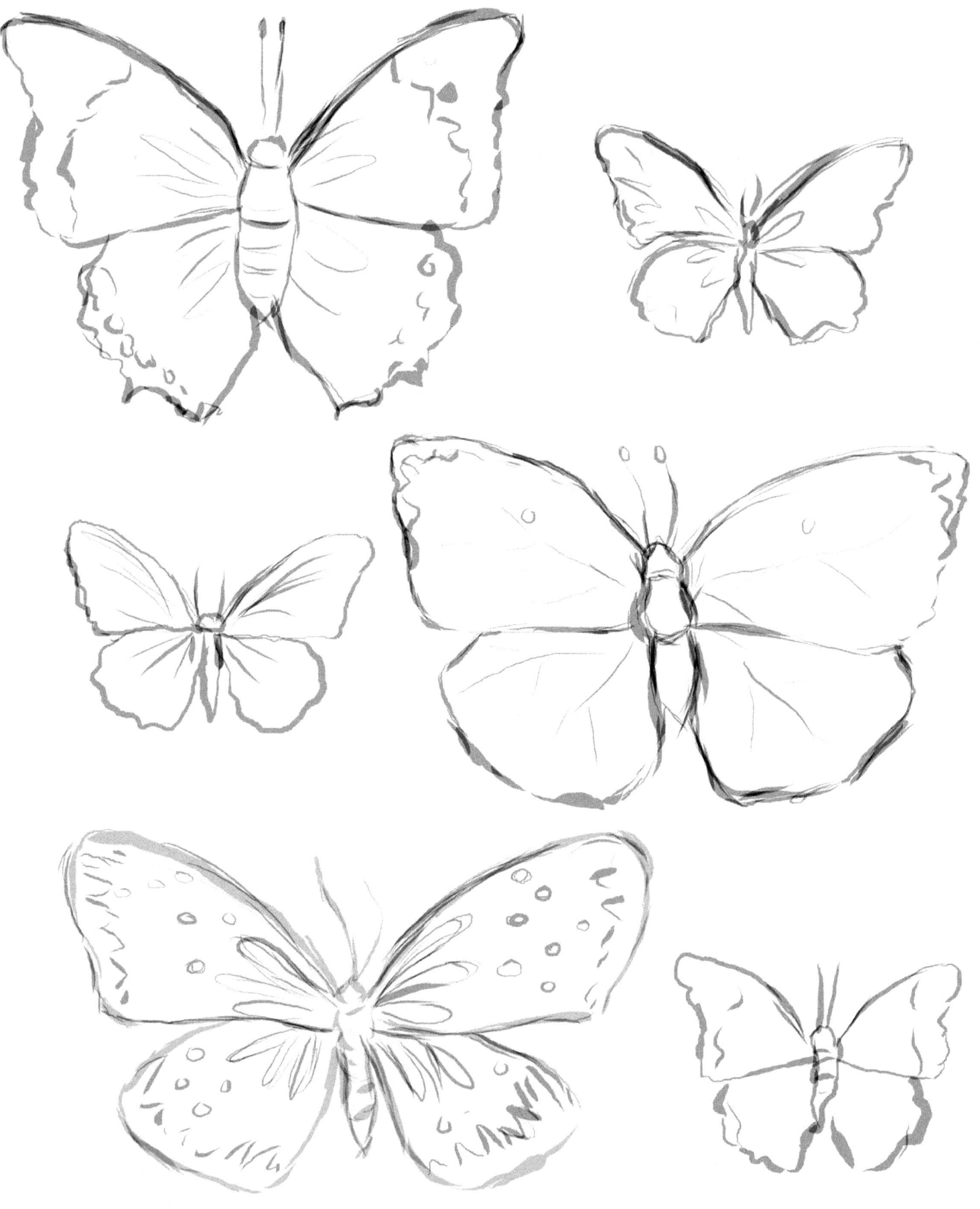

Believe

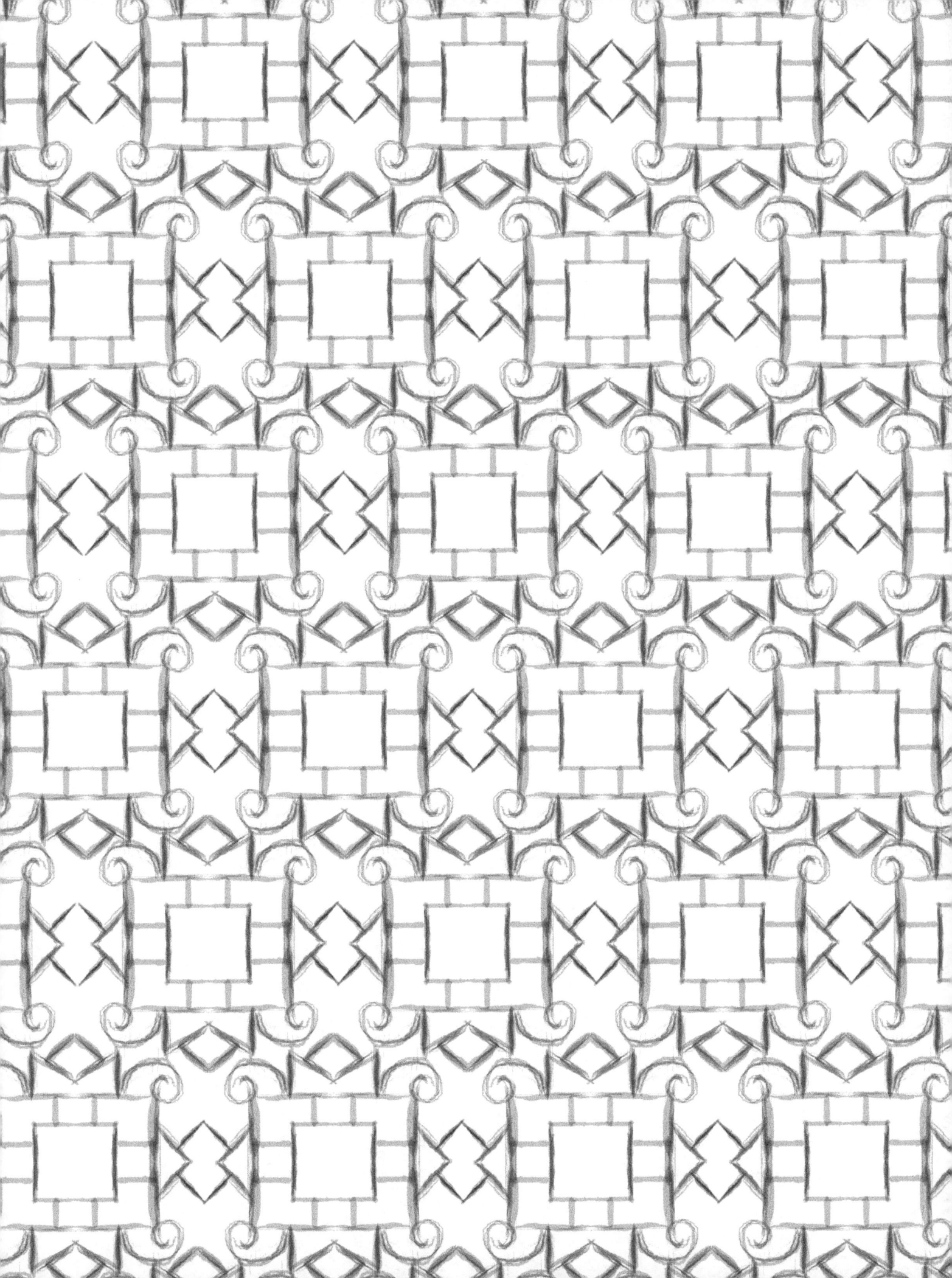

Believe

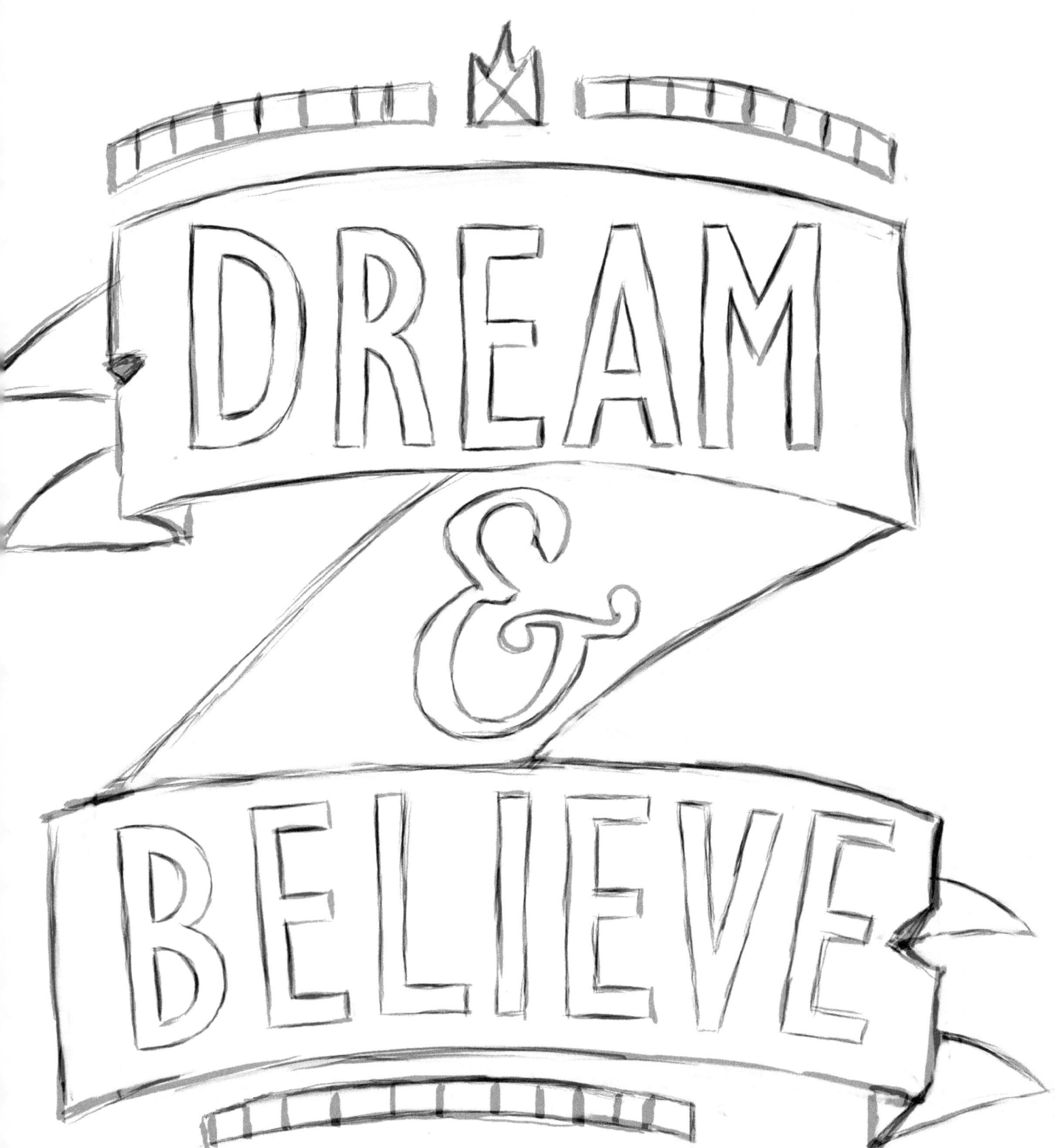

Believe